Wars Waged Under the Microscope

The War Against Smallpox

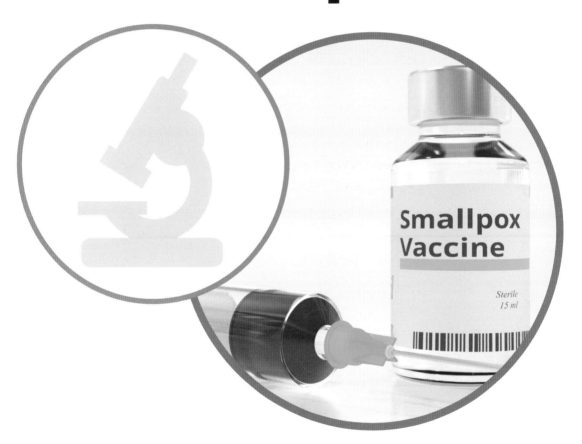

Louise Spilsbury

CRABTREE
PUBLISHING COMPANY
WWW.CRABTREEBOOKS.COM

CRABTREE
PUBLISHING COMPANY
WWW.CRABTREEBOOKS.COM

Author: Louise Spilsbury

Editors: Sarah Eason, Jennifer Sanderson, and Ellen Rodger

Editorial director: Kathy Middleton

Design: Simon Borrough

Cover design and additional artwork: Katherine Berti

Photo research: Rachel Blount

Proofreader: Wendy Scavuzzo

Production coordinator and Prepress technician: Ken Wright

Print coordinator: Katherine Berti

Consultant: David Hawksett

Produced for Crabtree Publishing by Calcium Creative Ltd

Photo Credits

Cover: Top right: James Gathany, Wikimedia Commons

Inside: Centers for Disease Control and Prevention: Dr. Paul B. Dean: p. 14; Robert Denty: p. 25; Shutterstock: Novikov Aleksey: p. 26; Design Cells: pp. 9, 12, 31; Dragon Images: p. 18; Everett Collection: pp. 4, 7, 16; Gorodenkoff: p. 27; Jearu: p. 6; Kateryna Kon: pp. 19, 28; Abel Echeverria Molinero: p. 13; Adi Purnatama: p. 20; Timonina: p. 15; Wellcome Images: Ernest Board/Wellcome Collection. Attribution 4.0 International (CC BY 4.0): p. 10; Wikimedia Commons: CDC: p. 22; CDC/James Gathanay: pp. 21, 24; CDC/James Hicks: p. 5; CDC/Brian Holloway: p. 8; CDC/World Health Organization/Stanley O. Foster: p. 23; James Gillray: p. 11; Philipp von Kapff: p. 17.

Library and Archives Canada Cataloguing in Publication

Title: The war against smallpox / Louise Spilsbury.
Names: Spilsbury, Louise, author.
Description: Series statement: Wars waged under the microscope | Includes bibliographical references and index.
Identifiers: Canadiana (print) 20210189169 | Canadiana (ebook) 20210189177 | ISBN 9781427151322 (hardcover) | ISBN 9781427151407 (softcover) | ISBN 9781427151483 (HTML) | ISBN 9781427151568 (EPUB)
Subjects: LCSH: Smallpox—Juvenile literature. | LCSH: Smallpox—Treatment—Juvenile literature. | LCSH: Smallpox—Prevention—Juvenile literature. | LCSH: Epidemics—Juvenile literature.
Classification: LCC RC183 .S65 2022 | DDC j614.5/21—dc23

Library of Congress Cataloging-in-Publication Data

Names: Spilsbury, Louise, author.
Title: The war against smallpox / Louise Spilsbury.
Description: New York, NY : Crabtree Publishing Company, [2022] | Series: Wars waged under the microscope | Includes index.
Identifiers: LCCN 2021016671 (print) | LCCN 2021016672 (ebook) | ISBN 9781427151322 (hardcover) | ISBN 9781427151407 (paperback) | ISBN 9781427151483 (ebook) | ISBN 9781427151568 (epub)
Subjects: LCSH: Smallpox--Juvenile literature. | Smallpox-Treatment--Juvenile literature. | Smallpox--Prevention--Juvenile literature. | Epidemics--Juvenile literature.
Classification: LCC RC183 .S69 2022 (print) | LCC RC183 (ebook) | DDC 614.5/21--dc23
LC record available at https://lccn.loc.gov/2021016671
LC ebook record available at https://lccn.loc.gov/2021016672

Crabtree Publishing Company
www.crabtreebooks.com   1-800-387-7650

Printed in the U.S.A./062021/CG20210401

Published in Canada
Crabtree Publishing
616 Welland Ave.
St. Catharines, Ontario
L2M 5V6

Published in the United States
Crabtree Publishing
347 Fifth Ave.
Suite 1402-145
New York, NY 10016

Contents

The Enemy

Smallpox was one of the biggest killers in the history of human illnesses. This deadly disease was caused by a *Variola* virus—a tiny organism too small to be seen by the unaided human eye. In the 1900s, medical science used all the tools at its disposal to fight this enemy.

A Deadly Disease

While most people who had smallpox recovered, about three out of every ten who contracted, or got, the disease died. People who contracted smallpox developed terrible blisters that filled with a sticky substance called pus.

The blisters swelled and burst, causing the pus to seep out. The disease was deadly to many, and those who survived were often badly scarred. Many were even blinded.

Smallpox gets its name from the pus-filled blisters, also known as pocks, which form during the illness.

The Story of Smallpox

In the 1700s, smallpox was the cause of death of around 400,000 people in Europe each year. The reign of terror of this disease lasted into the 1900s when, in that century, smallpox killed at least 300 million people worldwide. That is more than the total number of people who were killed during both World Wars.

Thankfully, today smallpox is no longer a threat, but the path to defeating this once-deadly killer has been long and hard. As with all deadly diseases, destroying the enemy has involved years of scientific study. The defeat of smallpox has been a major human victory—it is the only human disease that scientists and doctors have ever been able to **eradicate**. There have been no naturally occurring cases of smallpox since the 1970s.

This photograph of a young girl from Bangladesh shows how devastating smallpox was. Her entire face and body are covered with the pus-filled blisters that were typical of the disease.

"No man dared to count his children as his own until they had had the disease..."

Comte de la Condamine (1701–1774), mathematician and scientist

The Spread of Smallpox

No one knows how smallpox as a natural disease first began. One idea is that humans were infected by a *Variola*-like virus from **rodents** about 10,000 years ago or more.

A form of the smallpox virus may have passed from rodents to humans thousands of years ago, probably in Africa.

Conquering the World

The earliest physical evidence of smallpox that scientists have is scars from a **pox**-like rash on the **mummy** of Pharaoh Rameses V of Egypt, who died in 1157 BCE. Early cases of the disease spread around the world as populations grew and people traveled farther. **Traders** carried the disease from Egypt to India and, from there, it swept into China. By the 500s CE, it had reached Japan. Armies returning to Europe from overseas brought back smallpox in the 1000s and 1100s CE .

CASE STUDY: MASS DEVASTATION

Historians say that smallpox nearly wiped out the **Indigenous** populations in North, Central, and South America between 1500 CE and 1800 CE. When European settlers arrived in the Americas, they carried diseases such as smallpox. Indigenous peoples had never encountered those diseases before and so had no **immunity** against them.

In 1492, Italian explorer Christopher Columbus and his crewmen arrived on the shores of an island in the Bahamas that he named San Salvador. The local Taino people welcomed the foreign sailors. The first town that Columbus founded was on the island of Hispaniola, which is today shared between the Dominican Republic and Haiti. In 1492, the island had a population of at least 60,000 people. By 1548, there were fewer than 500 Taino left. Diseases, including smallpox, brought by the Europeans had caused widespread death.

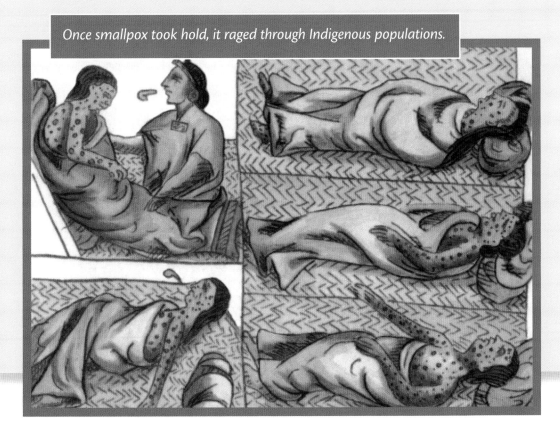

Once smallpox took hold, it raged through Indigenous populations.

The Battle Begins

Throughout history, when an **epidemic** of smallpox traveled through an area, some people survived. Then, when the disease returned, these survivors did not catch it again—they had become **immune** to smallpox. By recognizing this, people were able to use that knowledge to develop the first weapons against the disease.

First Steps to Victory

About 1,000 years ago, people in China and India observed that getting and recovering from smallpox protected children against any future **outbreaks** of the disease. So, they decided to infect people with mild smallpox on purpose to try to protect them from getting the disease in the future. They began to crush crusts of smallpox scabs into a powder, which healthy people breathed in through the nose. Alternatively, they scratched the skin and inserted smallpox pus or powdered scab into the wound.

Trying to Control the Disease

This first attempt at protecting against smallpox reached Europe and America in the 1700s, where it became known as variolation, after the Latin name for smallpox virus—*Variola*. The disadvantage of variolation was that people who had been given mild infections became carriers of the disease and could infect other people. This sometimes led to epidemics. It was also difficult to control how bad an infection the variolation would give. After variolation, some people had full-blown smallpox and died.

This Indian bottle contained live smallpox virus taken from active smallpox lesions to use for variolation.

UNDER THE MICROSCOPE

Variolation was devised after observing the effects of disease. It was only centuries later that scientists learned how the body's **immune system** fights viruses. When white blood **cells** in the blood recognize virus particles, they make substances called **antibodies** that attack the viruses. After the antibodies have attacked a virus, they stay in the blood, ready to destroy the same viruses if they get into the body in the future.

Antibodies destroy a cell that is infected by a virus. They get rid of the invading virus and stop an infection from spreading.

cell

antibody

Weapons Against Smallpox

While variolation and natural immunity helped, smallpox was still terrorizing the world in the 1700s. In the late 1700s, British surgeon Edward Jenner developed the first ever **vaccine** against an infectious disease. He gave the world its first real weapon against smallpox.

A Daring Discovery

Jenner had been **inoculated** with smallpox by variolation at the age of eight and later as a surgeon, but he was interested in finding a more powerful weapon against the disease. He noted that milkmaids who had suffered from cowpox, a disease they caught from the cattle they worked with, often had no reaction at all to smallpox variolation. After having cowpox, which was a much milder disease than smallpox and never deadly, they seemed generally immune to smallpox.

Jenner named his discovery Variolae vaccinae, *which is Latin for "smallpox of the cow." It wasn't until later that it later became known as a vaccine.*

Weapons Testing

Jenner decided to test if being given a dose of cowpox could protect people from smallpox. In May 1796, he inoculated a boy with cowpox. He scraped pus from cowpox blisters on the hands of a milkmaid who had caught cowpox, and injected the boy with the pus. A few months later, he gave the boy the smallpox virus by variolation. It worked. The boy did not develop any smallpox symptoms, or signs of illness, and was believed to be immune to smallpox.

Taking Action

After doing more tests on other children and gathering more proof, Jenner's theory and results were published, or made public through print, in 1798. Even though Jenner had proven his discovery worked, many people did not like the idea of injecting someone with material from a diseased animal. It was not until 1853, after a terrible smallpox epidemic, that the British government passed the **Vaccination** Act, which made smallpox vaccination **compulsory**.

This cartoon from 1802 illustrates the fears people had about the cowpox vaccine. It shows the vaccine being given to patients who then had cows emerging from their bodies!

"*Future nations will know by history only that the loathsome smallpox has existed and by you has been **extirpated**.*"

Former United States president Thomas Jefferson, letter to Edward Jenner, 1806

An Invisible Threat

Like other viruses, *Variola* virus particles, or pieces, are so small they can be seen only with the aid of a microscope. A microscope is a tool that magnifies, or makes bigger, tiny objects. The fact that viruses are otherwise invisible makes them very dangerous.

Virus Attacks

Viruses can reproduce, or make copies of themselves, only when they enter the cell of an animal or plant. The animal or plant that viruses live inside is called a host. The virus copies, then spreads out and starts to take over other cells. When viruses such as the *Variola* virus damage a host's cells, they cause disease.

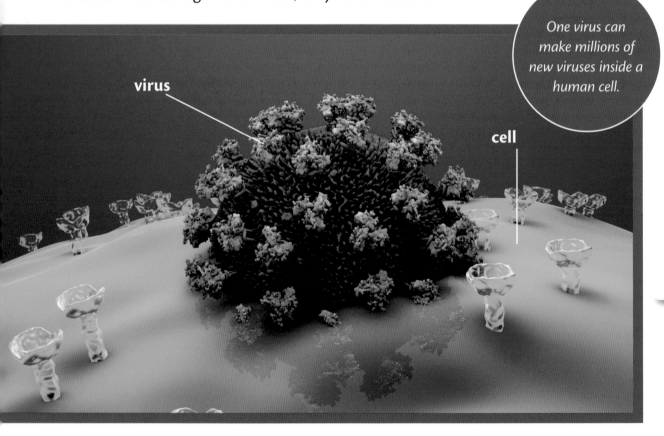

One virus can make millions of new viruses inside a human cell.

virus

cell

Viruses on the Move

The smallpox virus is highly contagious. That means it spreads rapidly from one person to another, then another. When someone with smallpox coughed, spoke, or sneezed, virus particles traveled through the air in saliva droplets, and other people breathed them in. The pus that oozed out of the sores of smallpox sufferers was infectious to anyone who touched it. Smallpox was also spread through contact with **contaminated** clothing and bedding.

UNDER THE MICROSCOPE

When the smallpox virus touches a cell, it injects part of itself into the cell or the cell swallows it up. Once inside, the virus takes over the parts of the cell that make the cell work. The virus uses them to make copies of itself. Eventually, there are so many copies of the original virus inside the host cell that it bursts.

Under Attack

When smallpox viruses took over a human host's cells, it was as though the body was under attack. The names given to this devastating disease in the past—pox, speckled monster, and red plague—give an idea of the pain and suffering it caused hundreds of millions of people.

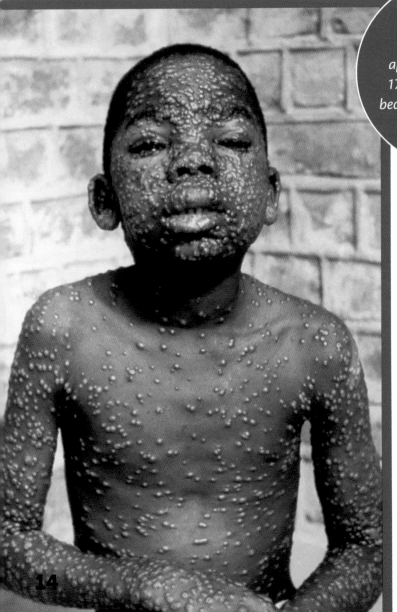

Pus-filled pimples, called pustules, appeared about 12 to 17 days after a person became infected with the smallpox virus.

Early Stages

Once a person was infected with the smallpox virus, it took between 7 and 17 days before the first symptoms of the disease appeared. In the **incubation period**, viruses took over more cells and multiplied. During that time, victims may not have known they had the disease and may have looked and felt healthy. At that stage, they were not contagious, so they could not infect other people.

Developing Symptoms

After the incubation period, patients developed symptoms, which included a **fever**, headache, and aches and pains. They felt extremely tired. Red spots appeared in their mouths and throat, on their faces, hands and arms, and later on their chests and abdomens. Within a day or two, many of those lesions turned into small blisters filled with clear fluid that then turned into thick pus. Scabs formed on those lesions eight to nine days later and eventually fell off. The lesions were very painful.

The most infectious period is during the first week of illness, although a person with smallpox is still infectious until the last scabs fall off.

Prisoners of the Pox

There was no cure for smallpox. Once a person was infected with the virus, they had to let the disease run its course. People who recovered from smallpox usually had severe scars, especially on their faces, arms, and legs. For those patients who died, death usually occurred 10 to 16 days after the start of symptoms.

Armed with Medicine

When people are vaccinated and develop immunity to a disease such as smallpox, the entire population benefits from the vaccination. Viruses have difficulty spreading when the majority of the population is immune. Eventually, the disease may disappear altogether. This is called herd immunity.

Herd Immunity

Vaccines are very safe and successful, but they do not always work for everyone. Some people cannot risk even a mild dose of a disease given as a vaccine. These include pregnant women and people with allergies, some skin conditions, and diseases that weaken the immune system. That is why the idea of herd immunity is so important. When a large number of people are vaccinated, this reduces the number of hosts that a smallpox virus can spread among. That means unvaccinated people have a very low risk of becoming infected. The virus stops being able to spread, because it has been reduced to a level that is too low to maintain.

Some early smallpox vaccinations were done by taking pus from a blister on one vaccinated person and using it to inoculate another person by scratching the material into their arm.

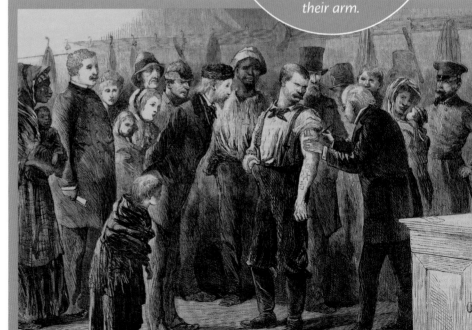

CASE STUDY: THE SPANISH VACCINE EXPEDITION

The Spanish smallpox vaccine **expedition** of 1803 became the first **immunization** campaign in the world. The expedition vaccinated at least 100,000 people and also taught doctors in Spanish colonies how to use the vaccine.

King Charles IV of Spain sent the first expedition to Latin America and the Philippines to provide the smallpox vaccine to as many people as possible. They also organized vaccination centers within areas controlled by the Spanish. Dr. Francisco Javier de Balmis led the campaign. He and his team took along boys who acted as living carriers for the vaccine—they passed it from the arm of one child to another until the ship arrived at its destination.

This statue depicts Dr. Francisco Javier de Balmis. During his journey, Balmis taught local doctors how to prepare, store, and use the smallpox vaccine.

Studying the Enemy

Although a vaccine for smallpox had been developed way back in the 1700s, no one knew what the virus looked like until centuries later. The powerful **electron microscope** was invented in 1931, so that scientists could actually see viruses in detail for the first time.

Microscopic Battles

Although scientists knew in the late 1800s that organisms, or living things, smaller than **bacteria** existed, they could not see them. Most virus particles are between 100 and 500 times smaller than bacteria, which makes them impossible to see under an ordinary microscope. Electron microscopes use a high-energy beam of **electrons** to help scientists see virus particles that are 50,000 times smaller than the width of a human hair.

Electron microscopes produce black-and-white images that are sometimes given a false color to make them easier to see. As well as more detail, electron microscope images also give a clear sense of the shapes and sizes of viruses.

Detailed Discoveries

Looking through their microscopes, **virologists** discovered that the cowpox and smallpox *Variola* viruses are members of the same family of viruses: the poxviruses. Today, they know that cowpox worked as a vaccine because the virus was almost identical to the smallpox virus. Scientists could also use electron microscopes to study how viruses behaved inside cells. They saw that poxviruses are unique among **DNA viruses** because they replicate, or copy themselves, in a different part of a cell.

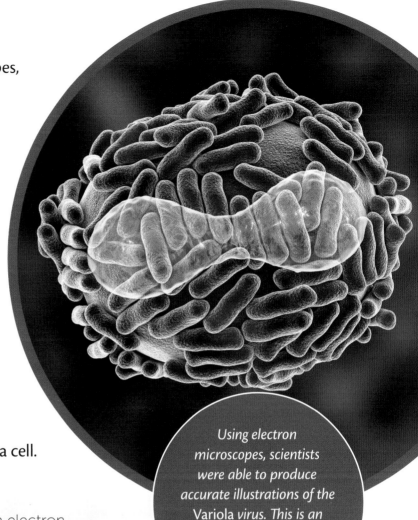

Using electron microscopes, scientists were able to produce accurate illustrations of the Variola virus. This is an artist's impression of a virus as seen under a microscope.

UNDER THE MICROSCOPE

Under an electron microscope, scientists could see smallpox *Variola* viruses in a cell and identify them by their shape and structure. The *Variola* virus particle is brick-shaped and consists of a **DNA (deoxyribonucleic acid)** genome surrounded by a network of **proteins**. A genome is made up of a set of instructions, called genes, for making and maintaining an organism, "written" using a chemical code called DNA.

A Battle Won

As well as new vaccines and a new bifurcated needle to deliver the vaccine, the battle for smallpox eradication was fought on several other fronts as health care workers prepared to vaccinate entire populations.

Armed with Education

A smallpox **surveillance** system was put in place. Weekly case reports were provided by health care workers. Teams were formed to investigate each outbreak, to vaccinate immediate contacts of case patients, and to record all cases of disease that they discovered. Health care workers used any transportation they could, including horseback, to get to **remote** villages. They trained local people to give the vaccinations. They used information campaigns and even songs and theater to educate the public about the disease and explain how vaccination worked. Health care workers also asked local people to report people who had smallpox symptoms. By 1971, smallpox was eradicated from South America, followed by Asia in 1975, and finally Africa in 1977.

On May 8, 1980, the 33rd World Health Assembly officially declared the world free of smallpox.

22

CASE STUDY: THE LAST CASE OF SMALLPOX

In late 1975, Rahima Banu Begum, a three-year-old girl from Bangladesh, was the last person in the world to contract naturally acquired smallpox, or smallpox not from a form of vaccination.

On October 16, 1975, an eight-year-old girl named Bilkisunnessa reported to the local Smallpox Eradication Program team that Rahima had the signs of smallpox. The team paid Bilkisunnessa, herself a victim of smallpox, a reward for her information. Then they **isolated** Rahima at home. They put guards outside her house 24 hours a day to ensure no one came or went, until Rahima was no longer infectious. They carried out a house-to-house vaccination campaign within a 1.5-mile (2.4-km) area of Rahima's home. They also visited every home, public meeting space, and school within 5 miles (8 km) to ensure the disease did not spread. Their efforts made sure Rahima, who survived, was the last person to catch smallpox.

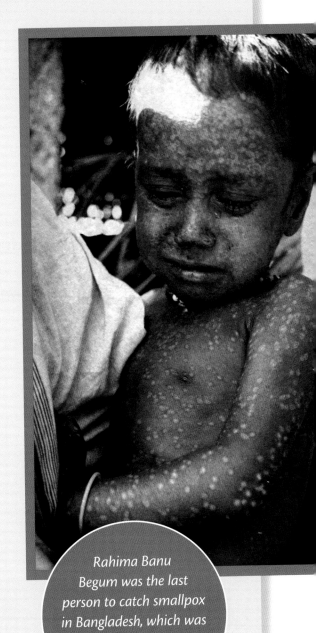

Rahima Banu Begum was the last person to catch smallpox in Bangladesh, which was declared smallpox-free on November 24, 1975.

New Weapons

Today, the smallpox *Variola* virus is kept in two secure laboratories, where scientists study it to see if they can come up with a cure. It is a case of keeping an eye on the enemy rather than letting it out of their sight.

Centers of Study

The two labs where stocks of *Variola* virus are stored and studied under WHO supervision are the Centers for Disease Control and Prevention (CDC) in Atlanta, Georgia, and the State Research Center of Virology and Biotechnology in Koltsovo, Russia. Studying the *Variola* virus helps scientists understand more about how smallpox and other pox viruses infect cells, and how the immune system responds to that infection.

The CDC high-containment facility in Atlanta runs 24 hours a day, 7 days a week, 365 days a year, while scientists try to find a cure.

Smart New Drugs

Scientists study the *Variola* virus to find better **antiviral** drugs that can reduce the harmful effects of smallpox. First, they look at each drug's ability to stop infection in a laboratory. Then they find out how the drug stops infection from happening. What they learn will help others understand how to stop *Variola* viruses from spreading and how to make better drugs to treat them.

Safer Vaccines

Vaccinia vaccines can cause **side effects** ranging from unpleasant to life-threatening, so researchers work to make new, safer vaccines. To test if they work, volunteers who agree to be vaccinated with new vaccines provide blood samples. The *Variola* virus is tested on these blood samples inside the secure laboratory. Sometimes, they are tested on mice and other animals in the lab, to get an idea of how well they might work on people.

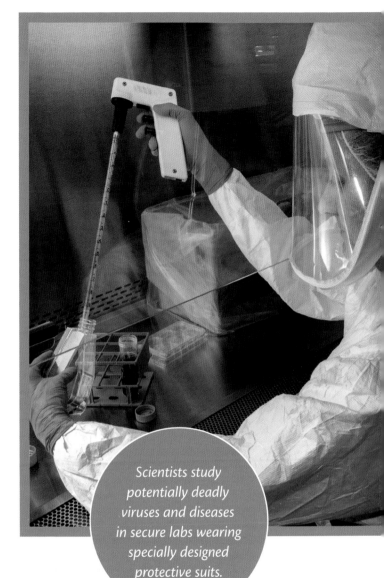

Scientists study potentially deadly viruses and diseases in secure labs wearing specially designed protective suits.

UNDER THE MICROSCOPE

In 2009, a team of researchers in Atlanta, proved how the smallpox *Variola* virus kills people. The team discovered that cells infected with *Variola* and a similar pox that affects monkeys, called monkeypox, produce a protein. This protein reduces the animals' immune systems' ability to stop viruses from reproducing.

Future Warfare

One important reason scientists continue to wage war against smallpox under the microscope is that there are fears this disease could be spread and used as a weapon in the future.

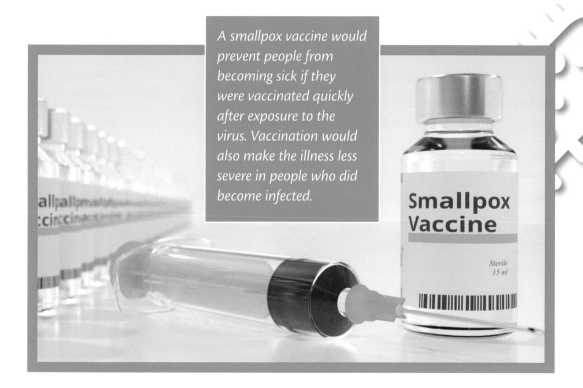

A smallpox vaccine would prevent people from becoming sick if they were vaccinated quickly after exposure to the virus. Vaccination would also make the illness less severe in people who did become infected.

Playing It Safe

Although it is best to be prepared, the reality is that it is very unlikely that anyone could use smallpox as a weapon. It is almost impossible to get hold of samples of the virus. The two research laboratories where they are held have security measures to guard against this. Even if samples of the *Variola* virus were obtained, it would be very difficult for anyone to make large amounts of the virus without being discovered. In the highly unlikely event that the smallpox virus did get out, scientists are working on new vaccines and antivirals. Countries also have supplies of the old vaccine. Because the *Variola* virus replicates slowly, people can still be successfully vaccinated up to four days after being exposed to it.

Learning from the Past

Virologists who study genomes of smallpox viruses may one day be able to tell us the origins of the smallpox virus that waged war against humans for thousands of years.

Scientists may learn even more about this microscopic enemy in the future. In 1990, scientists identified the genomes of different smallpox viruses. This helped them classify, or organize, viruses to investigate how they began, how they spread, and how they evolved, or changed over time. So far, virologists have only been able to study the genomes of *Variola* virus samples collected during the twentieth century. If samples of the virus particles can be collected from ancient remains, virologists may be able to finally solve the mystery of exactly when and how smallpox began.

> *"How did we cure polio, smallpox, and send a man to the moon? How did we decode the human genome in just 13 years? Collaboration."*
>
> **Margaret Cuomo, American doctor, author, campaigner and blogger on health issues**

Timeline

Smallpox was a deadly infectious disease that harmed people as far back as the days of ancient Egypt. Through scientific study and vaccination, it was successfully eradicated in 1980.

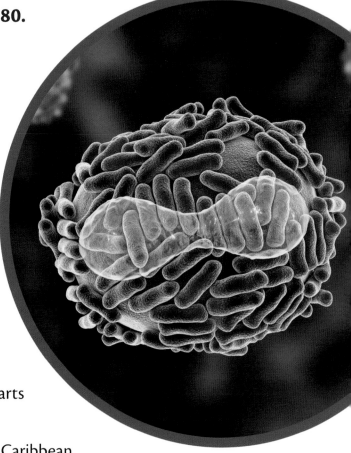

1157 BCE Pharaoh Rameses V of Egypt dies, probably from smallpox.

500s CE Trade with China and Korea introduces smallpox into Japan.

600s Smallpox spreads into northern Africa, Spain, and Portugal.

1000s Smallpox spreads farther in Europe.

1400s Portuguese settlers introduce smallpox into parts of West Africa.

1500s Smallpox spreads into the Caribbean, and Central and South America.

1600s Europeans bring smallpox to North America.

1700s Exploration by Great Britain introduces smallpox to Australia.

1700s	Smallpox kills more than 400,000 people in Europe each year.
1710s	People in Europe and America start to perform variolation to protect against smallpox.
1796	Edward Jenner invents the first smallpox vaccine.
1803	The Spanish smallpox vaccine expedition becomes the first immunization campaign in the world.
1853	The Vaccination Act makes smallpox vaccination compulsory in Great Britain.
1900s	Smallpox kills about 300 million people worldwide.
1950s	A higher-quality, freeze-dried smallpox vaccine is developed.
1960s	The bifurcated needle is developed to deliver the smallpox vaccine.
1967	The WHO starts a vaccination campaign to wipe out smallpox.
1971	Smallpox is eradicated from South America.
1975	Smallpox is eradicated from Asia.
1977	Smallpox is eradicated from Africa.
1980	The WHO officially declares the world free of smallpox.
1990	Scientists identify the genomes of different smallpox viruses.
2009	Researchers at the CDC in Atlanta prove how the smallpox *Variola* virus kills people.

Glossary

antibodies Substances produced by the body that fight off invading bacteria and viruses

antiviral Describes a drug that is effective against viruses

bacteria Single-celled organisms that can cause disease

cells The smallest units of a living thing that can survive on their own, carrying out a range of life processes

compulsory Required by law or rule

contaminated Dirty or infected

DNA (deoxyribonucleic acid) A part of the body's cells that gives each individual their own unique characteristics

DNA viruses Viruses in which the genetic material is DNA rather than a similar material called RNA

electron microscope A microscope that uses beams of electrons instead of rays of light

electrons Extremely small particles of matter with negative electrical charges

epidemic When many people in a community or country catch a disease at the same time

eradicate Completely get rid of

expedition A journey made by a group of people with a particular purpose

extirpated Completely destroyed

fever A high body temperature

freeze-dried Preserved by rapid freezing, then drying at a low temperature

historians People who study history

immune Resistant to a disease

immune system The organs and other parts of the body that work together to protect it against sickness

immunity A body's ability to stop a disease from affecting it

immunization The act of making a person or animal immune to infection, typically by inoculation

incubation period The period between exposure to an infection and the appearance of the first symptoms

Indigenous Describes people who were the original inhabitants of a region

inoculated Treated with a vaccine

isolated Kept separate from other people

lesions Wounds

mummy A dead body that has been treated and wrapped to prevent it from rotting

organism Living thing

outbreaks Infections of more than one person

pox Pockets of pus on the body

proteins Substances that do most of the work in cells

reconstituted Returned to its original state by adding water

remote Far away from major cities

rodents Small mammals, such as rats and gerbils, with sharp front teeth

side effects Unpleasant effects that taking a certain drug has on a person, such as making them feel dizzy

surveillance Close observation

traders People who buy and sell things

vaccination Giving a vaccine

vaccine A substance that helps protect against certain diseases

virologists Scientists who study viruses

virus A microscopic organism that can cause sickness

World Health Organization (WHO) An organization that helps governments improve their health services

Learning More

Find out more about smallpox and how the war against this deadly disease is being won.

Books

Goh, Hwee. *Invisible Enemies: A Handbook on Pandemics That Have Shaped Our World*. Marshall Cavendish International, 2020.

Hamen, Susan E. *The 12 Worst Health Disasters of All Time* (All-Time Worst Disasters). 12-Story Library, 2019.

Hand, Carol. *The Gross Science of Germs All Around You* (Way Gross Science). Rosen Central, 2018.

Havemeyer, Janie. *Smallpox: How a Pox Changed History* (Infected!). Capstone Press, 2019.

McCoy, Erin L. *Deadly Viruses* (The Top Six Threats to Civilization). Cavendish Square, 2019.

Websites

Discover more about smallpox at:
www.akronchildrens.org/kidshealth/en/kids/smallpox.html

Learn more about smallpox and vaccines against the disease at:
www.chop.edu/centers-programs/vaccine-education-center/vaccine-details/smallpox-vaccine

See a slideshow of historic smallpox images at:
www.nationalgeographic.com/science/health-and-human-body/human-diseases/smallpox

Find out more on the history of smallpox at:
www.sciencemuseum.org.uk/objects-and-stories/medicine/smallpox-and-story-vaccination

Index

ABOUT THE AUTHOR

Award-winning author Louise Spilsbury, who also writes under the name Louise Kay Stewart, has written more than 250 books for young people on a wide range of subjects. When not tapping away at her computer keys, she loves swimming in the sea and making bonfires on the beach near her home.